Editor: Jenny Corsey

Cover Design: Victoria DeJoy ● Graphic Design: Cecil Anderson and Lynette Rowe

Patriotic Favorites™

Hip! Hip! Hooray! For the U.S.A!

Published by

GALLOPADE™ INTERNATIONAL

800-536-2GET
www.gallopade.com

Gallopade is proud to be a member of these educational organizations and associations:

The National School Supply and Equipment Association (NSSEA)
American Booksellers Association (ABA)
Virginia Educational Media Association (VEMA)
Association of Partners for Public Lands (APPL)
Museum Store Association (MSA)
National Association for Gifted Children (NAGC)
Publishers Marketing Association (PMA)
International Reading Association (IRA)
Association of African American Museums (AAAM)

More Patriotic Books

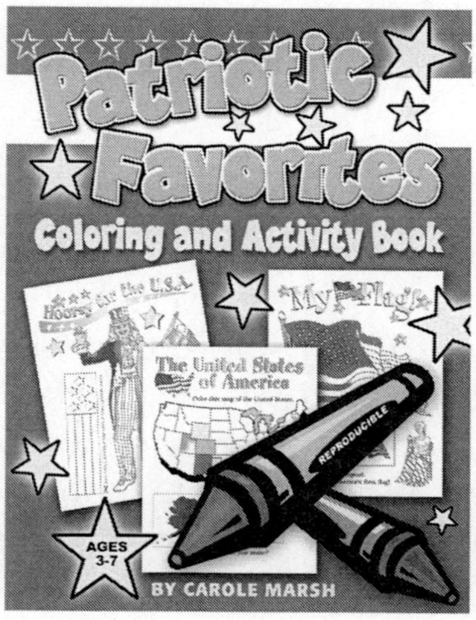

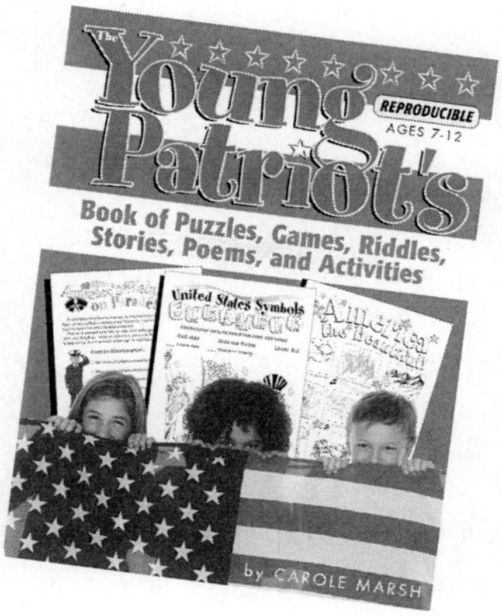

Readers™ about American Patriots
with many more to choose from!

A Word From the Author

Ever wonder what patriotism means? It means love for or devotion to one's country. A patriot is someone who gives of themselves for his or her country. And what's a biography, anyway? We usually think it is the life story of someone famous. When people achieve special goals, accomplish something significant in history, discover something that will help mankind, or create a work of art—we want to know more about those people. What they were really like. Why—and how—they did what they did. What that means to them, and to us. Would they do it again? Why or why not? What can we learn from their lives? I think the best biographies are about ordinary people. We may not even know their name, but their lives can be fascinating to us. Everyone has a biography (even a kid!)—a life story of what has happened to them and what they have done up till now. While you might think your biography is boring, it may be very exciting to someone who has lived an entirely different kind of life in a completely different type of place.

I like a biography that tells the truth. When we only learn the good side of the person, what they have done right, we don't learn how they accomplished things in spite of problems and failures. These are part of every life. Trial and error. Giving up. Starting over.

What can a kid learn from a biography? How other people have had to live their lives. And how they have chosen to live their lives. How everything you learn and do becomes part of the you that can often go on and do great things in spite of (and often because of!) a hard life, poverty, discrimination, handicaps, and other negative things that only you can turn to positive! You can learn that we're all pretty much alike. We have the same wants and hopes and dreams and fears and doubts. Some are smarter. Some have more money. Others may have more patience. Or determination.

You can learn that we're all pretty special. We all have something important to do while we're here on Earth. We may not know exactly what that is. We may never even find out. But when we can look and see how others may also have thought they had little to contribute, but made a great difference, even in the life of one other person—we can have hope that what we do is important, too.

In fact, the most important biographies have never (and probably never will) be written. If they were, they would be the biographies of our grandparents, our mothers, our fathers, our brothers and sisters, our aunts and uncles, our special friends, the teachers who helped us, the employer who gave us our first job, even our beloved pets.

After you read this book about some famous and not so famous patriots, I hope you will begin to look for biographies everywhere! In the newspaper, on television, in your schoolbooks, in letters, in conversations. After all, biographies are not written all at once. They are written like our lives. One day at a time.

Carole Marsh

George Washington [1732-1799]

George Washington is one of our most famous American patriots. He was born on February 22, 1732 in Pope's Creek, Virginia. George grew up in a large family on his father's tobacco farm. He loved to ride horses and play with his five brothers on the farm. George wanted to join the navy, but his mother didn't approve. He became a land surveyor. Later he joined the army of Virginia. During the French and Indian War, George fought bravely and was promoted to colonel.

When his older brother died, George inherited his house, Mount Vernon. Soon he met a pretty widow named Martha Custis, who had two young children. George and Martha married and lived peacefully at Mount Vernon. They loved to dance, attend concerts, and hunt. George raised horses, cattle, and sheep. He also grew apples, peaches, and pears.

Virginia elected George Washington to the House of Burgesses. High taxes and unfair laws from England, their mother country, angered the American colonists. George helped discuss the problem at the First Continental Congress. The colonists declared independence! They fought for their own free country. The American Revolution lasted for six years.

George Washington was named Commander of the American Continental Army. He encouraged his troops during the long war, especially when supplies and ammunition ran low. The soldiers often wore ragged clothing and did not have shoes, even during winter. They were hungry and tired, but they followed George's strong leadership. The American patriots won the war!

In Philadelphia, George presided over the Constitutional Convention. It met to write the first Constitution of the United States! In 1789, Americans elected George Washington, who received EVERY VOTE, president of the United States! He served two terms, which was eight years. During his presidency, he asked Americans to explore their new country and settle the west. George was asked to serve a third term, but he retired to Mount Vernon instead. George and Martha Washington lived together two more years before he caught a cold and died on December 14, 1799.

George Washington was one of America's greatest presidents and patriots. The capital of the United States, Washington, D.C., the Washington Monument, and many other places were named after him. Citizens remember him as "first in war, first in peace, and first in the hearts of his countrymen."

Benjamin Franklin [1706-1790]

Benjamin Franklin was born in Boston, Massachusetts on January 17, 1706. There were 17 children in his family, and Benjamin was the fifteenth! Benjamin worked in his father's candle shop, which he did not like. He wanted to be a sailor! He loved to read books about grammar, science, math, and language, but Benjamin's father could not afford to send him to school. His father helped him get into the printing business instead. At age 12, Benjamin signed a contract to work as an apprentice for his older brother James, a printer. He enjoyed printing but not working for James.

Benjamin ran away to Philadelphia, the largest colonial city at that time. For seven years, he worked for many different printers in Philadelphia and London, England. By 1730, Benjamin had married Deborah Read and owned his own print shop. He published the *Pennsylvania Gazette* newspaper and *Poor Richard's Almanac.* The book's clever sayings made Benjamin very popular.

In 1736, Benjamin was elected to the Pennsylvania Assembly, where he served for many years. Benjamin wanted Philadelphia to be a great city! He improved the mail system and planned for paved and lighted streets. He made sure there was a fire department, insurance company, city hospital, public library, and a night watch for security. Benjamin founded a school, which later became the University of Pennsylvania.

Then Benjamin entrusted the printing business to his foreman. He wanted to spend more time on his scientific experiments. He invented the Franklin stove, bifocal glasses, and the lightning rod–by flying a kite with an attached key during a thunderstorm! Benjamin's many scientific discoveries brought awards and honorary degrees from universities in Europe and America.

In 1754, Benjamin became a Pennsylvania delegate to the Continental Congress. He traveled to England to represent the colonies on important tax issues and stayed for several years. However, when the American Revolution began, Benjamin returned to support his American friends. In 1776, he sailed on another ambassador mission. He convinced France to help the colonists fight against England. He lived there nine years and negotiated trade treaties.

In 1785, Benjamin Franklin returned to America to live in Philadelphia. He became a Constitutional Convention member and helped draft the first constitution of the United States. He died on April 17, 1790. Americans remember Benjamin Franklin as a great scientist, writer, ambassador, printer, inventor, statesman, and devoted patriot!

Abraham Lincoln
[1809-1865]

Abraham Lincoln is perhaps America's favorite president. Historians voted him the greatest president in history. At 6'4" Abraham was even America's *tallest* president! His leadership and integrity set an example for citizens and politicians everywhere. Yet the presidency was not a simple task for him to achieve. He was uneducated, unattractive, poor, and without political connections. But he didn't give up!

Abraham Lincoln was born on February 12, 1809 on a Kentucky farm. His mother died when he was young. His father remarried a widow named Sarah. She had three children. Sarah loved the Lincoln family and shared a close friendship with Abraham. He called her "angel mother," and she encouraged his education. Abraham couldn't attend school because he worked all day to support his family. Since the family only owned a Bible, Abraham walked many miles to borrow books from other frontier families.

Abraham opened a store, but then he found an interesting law book. He later joined a law office in Springfield, Illinois. He married Mary Todd and raised four boys: Robert, Edward, William, and Thomas. Abraham loved to tell stories and play with his sons. When two of them died of illness, Abraham was heartbroken.

Abraham joined politics. He was defeated in the 1832 Illinois House of Representatives election, but won the 1834 race and was reelected three consecutive terms. He lost the 1843 U.S. House of Representatives race, but secured a House seat in 1846. Then Abraham lost the 1855 Senate race, lost the vice presidency in 1856, and lost another Senate race in 1858. After years of persistence, Abraham Lincoln was finally elected president of the United States in 1860!

Big problems greeted Abraham at the capital. Southern states had seceded from the Union and formed a Confederacy. When they attacked Fort Sumter in South Carolina, Abraham declared a Civil War had begun. In 1862, he delivered the Emancipation Proclamation to free U.S. slaves. He wrote a supporting constitutional amendment as well. After Union forces won the war, Abraham told the nation he wanted to restore peace quickly. Four days later, John Wilkes Booth shot Abraham Lincoln at Ford's Theater. John didn't like Abraham because he supported the Confederacy. He was bitter that his side had lost the war. The nation mourned the death of their president who had overcome great obstacles to bring great freedom to the people.

Legendary...

Gen. Omar N. Bradley [1893-1981]

- Five-star General, U.S. Army Chief of Staff, Chairman of the Joint Chiefs of Staff, led Veterans Administration
- Commanded U.S. ground troops in France during the 1944 D-Day invasion
- Known as "The Soldier's General" because of his compassion toward the men under his command

Gen. Dwight D. "Ike" Eisenhower [1890-1969]

- Five-star General and Chief of Staff of U.S. Army in World War II
- 34th U.S. president: first president to govern all 50 states
- Ended Korean War with truce agreement

Gen. Hiram Ulysses "Unconditional Surrender" Grant [1822-1885]

- 18th U.S. president, served two terms (eight years)
- Best Union general of Civil War
- Served in Mexican American War

Gen. Andrew "Old Hickory" Jackson [1767-1845]

- Fought in War of 1812; Battle of New Orleans hero
- 7th U.S. president
- U.S. representative, U.S. senator, superior court judge

Gen. Thomas "Stonewall" Jackson [1824-1863]

- Fought in Mexican American War
- Virginia Military Institute professor
- Confederate General in Civil War
- Nicknamed "Stonewall" for his steadfast gaze and posture

American Generals

Gen. Robert E. Lee [1807-1870]

- Confederate Army Commander, but opposed slavery and secession
- Fought in Mexican American War
- President of Washington and Lee College

Gen. Douglas MacArthur [1880-1964]

- General in World War I, won honors for leadership of 42nd "Rainbow" Division
- Led Allied troops in Pacific during World War II
- U.S Army Chief of Staff

Gen. George C. Marshall [1880-1959]

- Five-star General and U.S. Army Chief of Staff during World War II; helped plan D-Day invasion
- U.S. secretary of state; won Nobel Peace Prize for the Marshall Plan which rebuilt Europe after World War II
- Supervised Civilian Conservation Corps during Great Depression

Gen. George S. Patton Jr. [1885-1945]

- World War II General who commanded 3rd Army and liberated Buchenwald concentration camp
- Once jumped from a moving vehicle, on his way to a formal dinner in a tuxedo, to save a woman from being abducted by three men
- Competed in the 1912 Olympics at Stockholm, Modern Pentathlon

Gen. Colin L. Powell [1937–]

- Four-star general, and Chairman of the Joint Chiefs of Staff (highest military position in the Department of Defense)
- Oversaw Operation Desert Storm in the 1991 Persian Gulf War
- First African-American Secretary of State

Samuel Adams [1722-1766]
Samuel Adams founded the Sons of Liberty, a patriot group that organized public riots and acts of rebellions, such as the Boston Tea Party, to speak out against unfair British policies. Thomas Jefferson called Samuel "truly the Man of the Revolution." Samuel's efforts helped launch the American Revolution for independence. He also served in the First and Second Continental Congresses, was elected governor of Massachusetts, signed the Declaration of Independence, and helped draft the U.S. Constitution.

Ethan Allen [1738-1789]
Ethan Allen was born in 1738 in Litchfield, Connecticut. His dreams of a Yale University education were cut short when his father died in 1755. Ethan joined a local militia company, but later organized the "Green Mountain Boys" at Catamount Tavern in Bennington, Vermont. After the British declared him an outlaw, Ethan led the Green Mountain Boys to capture Fort Ticonderoga in 1775. British soldiers captured Ethan during a patriot attack on Montreal. After two years of imprisonment, Ethan was exchanged for the release of a British prisoner. Ethan fought for Vermont statehood after the war.

Clara Barton [1821-1912]
Clarissa "Clara" Barton changed careers when a wounded Union regiment wandered into Washington, D.C. She gave them bandages and left her job to beg for food and supplies for the soldiers. Clara sought donations everywhere and rented a warehouse space when her small apartment grew full. When Clara heard about a battle, she followed the army and worked without sleep delivering food and water to weary soldiers collapsed in the fields. Known as "The Angel of the Battlefield," Clara organized a program to find soldiers missing in action. She also convinced the U.S. to sign the Geneva Treaty, which provided relief for sick soldiers. Clara later founded the American Red Cross in 1881 and served as its first president.

William Jennings Bryan [1860-1925]
William Jennings Bryan, a three-time U.S. presidential candidate from Illinois, served the United States as a U.S. congressman, U.S. Army colonel, and U.S. secretary of state. Known as the "silver tongue orator," William also practiced law, edited the *Omaha World-Herald* newspaper, and maintained a deeply religious life. William also wrote several books and pamphlets on social and political issues. He served as lead prosecuting attorney for Tennessee state in the famous "Scopes Monkey Trial," which debated evolution instruction in schools.

John C. Calhoun [1782-1850]
John Caldwell Calhoun served nearly 40 years in the federal government, including offices such as U.S. congressman, U.S. secretary of war, U.S. senator, U.S. secretary of state, and U.S. vice president. The famous South Carolina patriot staunchly defended states' rights. He

practiced law, authored the South Carolina Exposition resolution, arranged the annexation of Texas, and helped lead the United States through the War of 1812 with the British.

Margaret Cochran [1751-1800]
Margaret Cochran traveled to the battlegrounds with her husband during the American Revolution. She bravely fought against British troops at the Battle of Fort Washington. When her husband died, she continued fighting until she suffered a severe wound herself. Margaret became disabled for life. She was the first woman in the United States to receive a pension.

Dorothea Dix [1802-1887]
At age 60, social reformer Dorothea Dix organized and managed all of the female nurses for the Union forces during the Civil War. She worked without pay every day of the four battle years, even when ill. Dorothea skipped meals, slept on floors, cared for tired nurses in her own home, organized fundraisers, created more hospitals, and even paid for an ambulance herself. Her inspections of hospitals in the North resulted in cleaner, safer conditions for wounded soldiers, who loved her and brought her baskets of flowers in gratitude.

Cornelia Fort [1919-1943]
Cornelia Fort of Tennessee was the first female pilot to die while serving her country. She was the second woman to volunteer for the Women's Auxiliary Ferrying Squadron (WAFS, later WASPs--Women Airforce Service Pilots). On the morning of December 7, 1941, Cornelia Fort nearly collided with a Japanese aircraft leaving Pearl Harbor while she flew with a student pilot. During World War II, she was killed in a mid-air collision when another plane struck hers on a routine transport. Her famous quote can be read on a marker at the Cornelia Fort Airport in Tennessee: "I am grateful that my one talent, flying, was useful to my country."

Alexander Hamilton [1757-1804]
Alexander Hamilton was born illegitimately on the island in the British West Indies to a poor merchant and a planter's daughter. The community discovered his intelligence and collected funds for his education. While studying at King's College, he wrote several popular pamphlets about patriot issues. When war erupted, Alexander fought as a lieutenant colonel. He later served as secretary and aide-de-camp to General Washington. After the war, he practiced law. He was elected to the Continental Congress, the Constitutional Convention, and the New York governorship. As the first U.S. secretary of the treasury, Alexander stabilized the new government's finances and established a national bank. He died from a mortal wound caused by a duel with Aaron Burr and was buried in Trinity Churchyard in New York City.

Patrick Henry [1736 -1799]
A native Virginian and one of our greatest patriots, Patrick symbolized the colonists' struggle for liberty and self-government during the American Revolution by protesting British tyranny

with his entire strength. Patrick was a skilled lawyer and legendary orator. His most famous words were: "I know not what course others may take; but as for me, give me liberty or give me death!" Patrick served in public office for nearly 30 years, including five terms as governor of Virginia. He was a member of the Virginia House of Burgesses and Continental Congress, and a delegate to the Virginia Convention and the Virginia Constitution Ratification Convention. Patrick's arguments against the Constitution helped create the Bill of Rights.

Thomas Jefferson [1743-1826]
Thomas Jefferson grew up in a wealthy Virginia family. While practicing law, he continued to enjoy a similar lifestyle at his lavish Monticello mansion. Thomas served as a Virginia legislator and governor, as well as an inventor. He helped give birth to the new nation of America when he wrote the Declaration of Independence. Thomas became John Adams' vice president in 1796. He was elected the third U.S. president four years later. During his two-term presidency, Thomas negotiated the Louisiana Purchase of 1803 with France, which doubled the size of America. He died on July 4, 1826, exactly 50 years after the Declaration of Independence was signed!

John Paul Jones [1747-1792]
Born in Scotland, John Paul Jones emigrated to the colonies and worked his way aboard a ship. He strongly supported the colonists' fight for freedom and became an avid patriot. As a captain in the American Navy, John declared, "I have not yet begun to fight," when ordered to surrender his ship to the British during the American Revolutionary War. Later known as the "Father of the American Navy," John Paul Jones died and was buried in France. He was later reburied at the U.S. Naval Academy in Annapolis, Maryland.

Lucius Quintus Cincinnatus Lamar [1825-1893]
Lucius supported Southern secession, but he desired peace and restoration after the Civil War. As a U.S. senator, he later delivered a heartfelt speech to Congress: "On both sides we must most earnestly desire to be one…in feeling and in heart…My countrymen! Know one another and you will love one another." His address helped heal a troubled and torn relationship between the North and South.

Richard Henry Lee [1732-1794]
Virginian Richard Henry Lee rose before a congress of delegates on June 7, 1776 to declare: "The united colonies are, and of right ought to be, free and independent States." He was the first to publicly declare the need for independence. The colonists debated his call, then passed the resolution. Five men were chosen to write a formal announcement: Benjamin Franklin, John Adams, Robert E. Livingston, Roger Sherman, and Thomas Jefferson. On July 1, the congress again debated the declaration, which the committee had produced, and voted to accept it the next day. John Hancock signed the original copy on July 4, followed by all 56 delegates.

Clare Booth Luce [1903-1987]
Clare Booth Luce led such a patriotic and successful life that she was named "Woman of the Century" after her death. She operated the Time-Life publishing empire with her husband, served as a U.S. congresswoman from Connecticut, wrote books and news articles, edited *Vanity Fair* magazine, crafted award-winning plays, and raised children! She was also the U.S. ambassador to Italy, and was one of the first women appointed to a major diplomatic post. Her foreign journalism included books and risky on-location articles about World War II.

James Madison [1751-1836]
James the Great Little Madison measured only 5'4" tall and weighed 100 pounds! He graduated from Princeton University two years early, then served as a Virginia delegate to the Continental Congress. James helped the delegates work together and compromise to form a constitution that everyone liked. He is called the "Father of the Constitution." After serving as U.S. secretary of state, James was elected the fourth U.S. president and served two terms, eight years. James and his wife Dolley remained active in politics and public affairs after his presidency had ended. They are still remembered as one of America's favorite couples.

George Mason [1725-1792]
George Mason learned about law by reading in his Uncle Henry's library of 1,500 books. He farmed the family land, practiced law, and served in the Virginia House of Burgesses. His speaking and writing talents became evident at the Virginia Constitutional Convention when he wrote and presented the Virginia Declaration of Rights. This document later became the basis for the Bill of Rights of the U.S. Constitution. He attended the U.S. Constitutional Convention of 1787 and delivered 136 speeches. However, he refused to sign the final version of the constitution because he did not believe it protected enough of the people's rights.

"Spark" Masayuki Matsunaga [1916-1990]
Masayuki Matsunaga was born on the island of Kauai in Hawai'i. He joined the 100th Infantry Battalion in the U.S. Army during World War II with 1,500 other Japanese American volunteers. His bravery in combat resulted in two Purple Hearts and a Bronze Star. He served as a U.S. senator for 14 years and fought for redress of Japanese-Americans unjustly interned during the war. He also sponsored legislation to establish the U.S. Peace Institute.

Major Samuel McColloch [1756-1782]
Major Samuel McColloch, a Virginia settler, commanded Ft. Van Metre (later called Ft. Henry) during the American Revolution. According to legend, he narrowly escaped an Indian ambush by leaping off a cliff into Short Creek on horseback. Both he and the horse survived! This place is now called "McColloch's Leap." Indians later killed Samuel during another ambush. Legend also says the Indians cut out his heart and ate it because they thought they would receive his bravery, loyalty, and skill!

Sandra Day O'Connor [1930 -]
In 1981, Sandra Day O'Connor became the first female U.S. Supreme Court justice. She grew up on an Arizona ranch without electricity or running water. Sandra graduated magna cum laude from Stanford University, and was the first female majority state senate leader. She founded the Arizona Women Lawyers Association and National Association of Women Judges.

Thomas Paine [1737-1809]
Thomas Paine wrote fiery words of revolution that spurred colonists on toward rebellion against the British in his famous pamphlet, Common Sense. It sold nearly 500,000 copies. By giving printing rights to the colonist government, Thomas donated nearly one million dollars in sales to the cause! His brave and blunt ideas rallied the colonists to the cause of American independence. The patriot argued that remaining loyal to England was impractical, morally wrong, and increasingly difficult. He urged colonists everywhere that now "tis time to part!"

Molly Pitcher [early 1750s-1832]
During the American Revolution and Civil War, many women fought with their husbands. During the American Revolution, Mary "Molly" Hays joined her husband, William, in battle. She carried a water pitcher to give relief to soldiers, who called her "Molly Pitcher." When William died at the Battle of Monmouth in 1778, Molly fired his cannon at the British! In 1822, legislators awarded her an annual lifetime pension for brave service.

Eleanor Roosevelt [1884-1963]
Eleanor Roosevelt was the most active first lady in U.S. history, a tireless humanitarian, and a political and social role model for women. Relatives raised her when she was orphaned. She married Franklin D. Roosevelt in 1905 and raised six children. Though Franklin admitted to an affair with her secretary, Eleanor chose not to leave him. When polio crippled Franklin, Eleanor remained an encouraging partner to him. She visited sick World War I veterans and volunteered. She grew more politically active by joining the Women's Trade Union League and directing the Democratic National Committee's Bureau of Women's Affairs. When Franklin was elected U.S. president, Eleanor became the first lady. She made unheard of impromptu public speeches in support of her husband, wrote books and a syndicated column, and helped found the National Youth Administration. Eleanor also toured the South Pacific to boost soldier morale, became a United Nations delegate and Human Rights Commission chairperson.

Theodore "Teddy" Roosevelt [1858-1919]
Theodore Roosevelt was a U.S. president who fought for social reform. He was born a sickly, timid child into a wealthy New York family. "Teddy" read books of fearless heroes and desired to match their courage! He studied academics, hunted big game, and exercised to improve his physique. When he entered politics, Theodore worked tirelessly to reform corrupt government. He boldly threw corrupt politicians and police from office, paying no mind to the effects on his own political career. During the Spanish American War, Theodore led the First U.S. Volunteer

Cavalry "Rough Riders" into battle. After victories at Kettle Hill and San Juan Hill, Theodore returned home to cheering crowds. He easily won the New York governorship. Later as U.S. vice president, Theodore became president when McKinley was assassinated in 1901. He advanced the growing reform movement to improve life for middle and lower class Americans, who loved his integrity. During his presidency, Theodore won the 1905 Nobel Peace Prize for mediating a peace treaty between Russia and Japan. Once he survived a bullet wound from an attempted assassination while delivering a speech and finished his oration while he bled. He also played football on the White House lawn and led a Boy Scout troop on Long Island. His six children loved pets and owned dogs, cats, squirrels, raccoons, rabbits, guinea pigs, a badger, a pony, a rat, a parrot, a green garter snake, and even a black bear cub!

Betsy Ross [1752-1836]
Elizabeth "Betsy" Ross was born on January 1, 1752 in Philadelphia. Betsy learned to sew and apprenticed for an upholsterer. When the American Revolution began, Betsy's husband John joined the Pennsylvania militia, but an explosion killed him. George Washington asked Betsy to sew a flag for the new nation. She created a flag with 13 alternating red and white stripes, to symbolize the 13 colonies. In the upper left corner, she added a patch of blue with 13 white stars in a circle. In 1777, the Continental Congress adopted the new American flag!

Roger Sherman [1721-1793]
Roger Sherman was born in Massachusetts. He apprenticed to a shoemaker, but he read books during every spare moment at work. When Roger turned 19, his father died and left the family in his care. After moving to Connecticut, Roger's exceptional mathematical skill landed him a surveyor's appointment. Roger practiced law and served as a judge and New Haven mayor. When elected to the general assembly of Connecticut, Roger fully supported the patriot cause. He signed the Declaration of Independence, Articles of Confederation, and U.S. Constitution. He was a U.S. representative and senator and presented the Connecticut Compromise at the Constitutional Convention.

Gen. John Stark [1728-1822]
General John Stark, a New Hampshire native, is among the most famous soldiers in U.S. history. He fought with Rogers' Rangers in the French and Indian War, served with the Vermont militia at the Battle of Bennington, and became the hero of Bunker Hill. General Stark's life spanned the entire revolutionary period, and his effective leadership help propel the nation toward independence. Many Americans today live by his famous patriotic words, "live free or die" (also New Hampshire's motto). When General Stark died in 1822, he was the last surviving Continental general of the Revolution.

Daniel Webster [1782-1852]
Daniel Webster was born in New Hampshire. A Dartmouth College graduate, Daniel practiced law and was elected a U.S. congressman and U.S. senator. His first public speech

took place on July 4, 1800. Daniel became one of America's greatest orators. Several of his speeches were legendary, especially when he defended the U.S. Constitution. Daniel was the first man elected to the U.S. Senate Hall of Fame. The Massachusetts legislature nominated him for the presidency, but Daniel lost. He was U.S. secretary of state under three presidents.

John Witherspoon [1723-1794]
John Witherspoon was born in Scotland. The brilliant prodigy attended the University of Edinburgh at age 13. When he moved to Philadelphia in 1769, he served as president of the College of New Jersey (now Princeton). He raised funds to save the school from bankruptcy, taught classes, reformed curriculum, wrote books, and founded a grammar school. At Princeton, he educated a future U.S. president and vice-president, nine cabinet officers, 21 senators, 39 congressmen, three Supreme Court justices, 12 state governors, and hundreds of clergyman, pastors, and missionaries. When the revolution erupted, John hoped the colonists and British could solve their differences. However, when England tried to install an Anglican bishop over the American colonies, John, also a Presbyterian minister, knew that their religious freedom was in danger. New Jersey elected John to the Continental Congress in 1776. He was so politically active that King George III once called the revolution, "that Presbyterian parson's war." As the only clergyman to sign the Declaration of Independence, John Witherspoon believed that political and spiritual freedom were inseparable. He is famous for saying, "He is the best friend to American liberty, who is most sincere and active in promoting true and undefiled religion."

George Wythe [1726-1806]
George Wythe was an accomplished Virginia statesman and patriot of the United States. He practiced law and became the first professor of law in the U.S. (College of William and Mary). George served in the Virginia House of Burgesses, Second Continental Congress, and Constitutional Convention. He was elected mayor of Williamsburg and Chancellor of Virginia. George used his legal wisdom to help write the Virginia constitution and the original Virginia protest against the Stamp Act. He signed the Declaration of Independence, helped design the Virginia state seal, and even played classical music in his spare time!

Sergeant Alvin York [1887-1964]
Sergeant Alvin York is often regarded as the greatest American patriot of World War I. Born in Tennessee, Alvin grew up poor. A religious pacifist, Alvin did not want to fight, but was drafted. An excellent marksman, Alvin was promoted to corporal. During the war, Alvin and 16 soldiers moved behind enemy lines by accident after misreading a map. In confusion, a large German company surrendered to them after a short exchange of bullets. Once the Germans saw they outnumbered their captors, they opened fire again. Alvin shot the machine gunner and the nine remaining Americans captured 132 prisoners. After the war, Alvin returned home to join politics and help educate poor children of Tennessee. Alvin did not want fame, but filmmakers pursued his story until he finally agreed to the idea. *Sergeant York* became one of the most successful films of the war era.

Great State Patriots

ALABAMA

- ★ **Alva Smith Belmont**, women's suffragist who founded the Political Equality Association
- ★ **John Hunt Morgan**, Confederate general
- ★ **Joseph "Fighting Joe" Wheeler**, Confederate Army officer, U.S. representative

ALASKA

- ★ **William A. Egan**, president of Alaska's constitutional convention, first elected governor in Alaska
- ★ **Ernest Gruening**, territorial governor of Alaska Territory who worked hard for statehood; U.S. senator
- ★ **William Seward**, U.S. secretary of state who negotiated purchase of Alaska with Russia

ARIZONA

- ★ **Sharlot Hall**, wrote a poem in 1905 that sparked the people's drive to become a state (she was only 12 years old!) and served as state historian
- ★ **Carl Hayden**, served in U.S. Congress for 57 years; his wife Nancy sewed the state's first flag
- ★ **Silvestre Herrera**, only Arizonan to win the Medal of Honor during World War II
- ★ **Charles DeBrille Poston**, "Father of Arizona," first territorial delegate to the U.S. Congress

ARKANSAS

- ★ **Augustus Hill Garland**, governor of Arkansas, U.S. senator, U.S. attorney general, first Arkansan appointed to a U.S. cabinet position
- ★ **General James Miller**, territorial governor of Arkansas Territory
- ★ **Loreta Janeta Velazquez**, Confederate widow who disguised herself as "Harry T. Buford" to command the "Arkansas Grays" unit (which she organized and funded); wounded twice as a soldier and Rebel spy

CALIFORNIA

- ★ **Gen. James H. Doolittle**, Air Force general
- ★ **Major General John C. Frémont**, pioneer who led first U.S. government explorations into California
- ★ **Robert Semple**, led Bear Flag Revolt, president of California's constitutional convention
- ★ **Earl Warren**, attorney general of California, three-term governor of California; U.S. Supreme Court chief justice, wrote 1954 ruling which outlawed racial segregation in public schools, and helped ensure rights of criminal suspects in *Miranda vs. Arizona* case
- ★ **Ronald Reagan**, actor, two-time California governor, 40th U.S. president (reelected)

COLORADO

- ★ **Ben Nighthorse Campbell**, U.S. representative and senator, first Native American senator from Colorado
- ★ **Catherine Murat**, "Mother of Colorado," first in Denver to fly the American flag, which she made from clothing

CONNECTICUT

- ★ **Nathan Hale**, American patriot soldier executed by the British as a spy, well known war martyr of the American Revolution famous for saying, "I only regret that I have but one life to lose for my country."
- ★ **Isaac Hull**, naval officer, served in undeclared naval war with France and the Tripolitan War, commanded *USS Constitution* "Old Ironsides" during the American Revolution, and defeated enemy company aboard the British *Guerrière* ship in the War of 1812
- ★ **William Samuel Johnson**, signed U.S. Constitution
- ★ **Israel Putnam**, major general in Continental Army, famous for shouting, "Don't fire until you see the whites of their eyes!" at the Battle of Bunker Hill

DELAWARE

- ★ **John Dickinson**, "penman" of the Revolution who wrote numerous pamphlets arguing against British colonial policies
- ★ **Colonel John Haslet**, led "Blue Hen's Chickens" regiment in the Revolutionary War
- ★ **Thomas McKean**, lawyer, first among Delaware's statesmen to favor American independence from England
- ★ **George Read**, lawyer who voted against separation from England but later signed the Declaration of Independence
- ★ **Caesar Rodney**, lawyer and landowner who cast tie-breaking vote in the Delaware delegation favoring independence from England

FLORIDA

- ★ **Gen. Joseph W. Stilwell**, one of the top U.S. army generals in World War II, earned Legion of Merit and Distinguished Service Medal, honored on U.S. stamp
- ★ **Gen. Charles Pelot Summerall**, U.S. army general of World War I, Citadel president

GEORGIA

- ★ **Lucius DuBignon Clay**, commander-in-chief of U.S. armed forces in Europe, military governor of U.S. military zone in Germany
- ★ **John Brown Gordon**, Confederate Army general, U.S. senator, governor of Georgia
- ★ **Button Gwinnett**, acting governor of Georgia, signed the Declaration of Independence, member of the Continental Congress
- ★ **Joseph Habersham**, served in Georgia convention to ratify U.S. Constitution, member of Continental Congress, U.S. Postmaster General
- ★ **Lyman Hall**, governor of Georgia, signed the Declaration of Independence, member of the Continental Congress
- ★ **Nancy Hart**, patriot who fought British troops during American Revolution and provided refuge for patriots in her north Georgia cabin
- ★ **Gen. Courtney Hicks Hodges**, four-star general, commanded American First Army in World War II
- ★ **Susie King Taylor**, freed slave who nursed black Union troops, taught them to read and write; worked without pay for four years; provided the only written record of a black Civil War nurse; organized the Boston branch of the Women's Relief Corps

- ★ **George Walton**, governor of Georgia, signed Declaration of Independence and Articles of Confederation

HAWAI'I

- ★ **Daniel K. Inouye**, U.S senator, World War II veteran, first Japanese American elected to Congress
- ★ **William F. Quinn**, territorial governor of Hawai'i, first state governor of Hawai'i

IDAHO

- ★ **William Edgar Borah**, trial lawyer, famous U.S. senator
- ★ **Pete Cenarrusa**, served nine consecutive terms as state representative, longest serving official in Idaho history
- ★ **Fred T. Dubois**, U.S. senator who led fight for Idaho's statehood

ILLINOIS

- ★ **Mary Ann "Mother" Bickerdyke**, cleaned up dirty Union hospitals and cared for wounded soldiers; often walked battlegrounds with a lantern at night to check for soldiers who might still be alive
- ★ **Nathan Heald**, commanding officer of Fort Dearborn who fought with his wife
- ★ **Mary Todd Lincoln**, wife of President Abraham Lincoln; raised money for Union war effort, homeless escaped slaves, and Civil War refugees; visited wounded soldiers
- ★ **Mary Ashton Rice Livermore**, organized women to help improve sanitary conditions for soldiers during the Civil War, traveled to battlefields and cities and then wrote about her discoveries, smuggled an abused seven-year-old slave to safety in her suitcase, kept a notebook with messages from parents to distribute to their soldier sons
- ★ **Ely Parker**, Native American military aide to Gen. Ulysses S. Grant during Civil War; wrote terms of surrender that officially ended war

INDIANA

- ★ **Ambrose Everett Burnside**, U.S. senator, governor of Rhode Island, inventor; commanded Army of the Potomac during Civil War
- ★ **Ernest Taylor Pyle**, popular war journalist during World War II, won Pulitzer Prize in 1944 for foreign correspondence; killed in action during the Okinawa campaign
- ★ **Lewis Wallace**, fought in Mexican War, blocked Confederate soldiers from capturing Washington, D.C. during Civil War as major general; wrote *Ben-Hur* novel

IOWA

- ★ **Mamie Doud Eisenhower**, popular First Lady, wife of president Dwight D. Eisenhower
- ★ **Annie Wittenmeyer**, provided better diets for sick and wounded soldiers in military hospitals during the Civil War and saved lives
- ★ **Grant Wood**, America's painter laureate, created famous *American Gothic* painting

KANSAS

- ★ **William "Buffalo Bill" Cody**, U.S. Army scout, Express Rider

- ★ **Charles Curtis**, U.S. representative, U.S. Senate majority leader, U.S. vice president
- ★ **Bob Dole**, U.S. representative and senator from Kansas, 1996 presidential candidate, wounded military veteran

KENTUCKY

- ★ **Ella Bishop**, rescued Union flag from vandalizing Confederate soldiers at age 17 in Lexington by wrapping it around her body and declaring that she would die before surrendering it; soldiers consented to her demands
- ★ **Daniel Boone**, explorer, hunter, pioneer, helped found and settle Kentucky
- ★ **Jim Bowie**, frontiersman, died fighting for the Alamo, invented Bowie knife
- ★ **Margaret E. Breckinridge**, Union nurse who cooked, sang hymns, and dressed wounds for wounded soldiers; responded to warning of death by exhaustion by saying: "Well, what if I do? Shall men come here by tens of thousands and fight and suffer and die, and shall not some women be willing to die to sustain and succor them?"
- ★ **Jefferson Davis**, president of Confederate States of America, Mexican American War hero, U.S. congressman and senator
- ★ **Monk Estill**, slave who used quick thinking to save the Estill's Station fort from Indian attack; he was rewarded with his freedom
- ★ **James Harrod**, Revolutionary War leader, surveyor, frontiersman
- ★ **Isaac Shelby**, first governor of Kentucky, member of the Patriot Militia during the American Revolution

LOUISIANA

- ★ **Jordan Noble**, young African American drummer who rallied American troops during the Battle of New Orleans.
- ★ **Bernard E. Randolph**, U.S. Air Force general
- ★ **Joseph Savary**, first African American commissioned as a military officer, served as major during the War of 1812

MARYLAND

- ★ **Franklin Buchanan**, naval officer in Mexican American War and Civil War, first superintendent of U.S. Naval Academy
- ★ **Charles Carroll**, signed Declaration of Independence, one of Maryland's first U.S. senators
- ★ **Frederick Douglass**, escaped slave, author, famous orator and abolitionist
- ★ **Barbara Frietchie**, ninety-year-old Union supporter who rescued a flag from Rebel soldiers and waved it defiantly before them out of her attic window!
- ★ **John Hanson**, Continental Congress member, first Congress of Confederation president
- ★ **Reverdy Johnson**, U.S. senator and U.S. attorney general who encouraged Maryland to remain in the Union before the Civil War
- ★ **Thurgood Marshall**, lawyer, first African American U.S. Supreme Court associate justice, received NAACP's Spingarn Medal
- ★ **Roger Taney**, U.S. attorney general, U.S. secretary of the treasury, U.S. Supreme Court chief justice
- ★ **Harriet Tubman**, former slave who risked her life to help 300 slaves, including her parents, escape to freedom on the Underground Railroad; served as Union army spy

MAINE

- ★ **Hannibal Hamlin**, governor of Maine, U.S. senator, U.S. vice president under Abraham Lincoln
- ★ **Gen. Oliver Otis Howard**, served in Civil War, founded Howard University, U.S. Military Academy president
- ★ **Rear Admiral William Kimball**, commanded first torpedo boat flotilla in Spanish American War
- ★ **Gen. Henry Knox**, first U.S. secretary of war
- ★ **Henry Wadsworth Longfellow**, poet and author, wrote "Paul Revere's Ride"
- ★ **Samantha Smith**, Augusta schoolgirl who asked Soviet Premier of Russia for world peace and was invited to visit his country!
- ★ **Rev. Samuel Francis Smith**, wrote "My Country 'Tis of Thee" lyrics
- ★ **Hannah Weston**, Revolutionary War heroine, carried 50 pounds of lead and powder with her sister to the *Margaretta*, a British ship which colonists destroyed

MASSACHUSETTS

- ★ **Abigail Adams**, first lady of second U.S. president John Adams; active women's rights advocate, prolific writer
- ★ **Louisa May Alcott**, wanted to fight in the Civil War so badly she secretly cried in her attic; wrote war stories and other books, volunteered for soldier's aid society, worked in Army Nursing Corps in a military hospital
- ★ **Benjamin Edes**, journalist who helped plan Boston Tea Party and co-founded pro-Patriot publication *Boston Gazette and Country Journal* in 1775
- ★ **John Hancock**, Continental Congress member, first to sign the Declaration of Independence
- ★ **Charles Lee**, Continental Army general during Revolutionary War, fought in Battle of Fort Sullivan
- ★ **Benjamin Lincoln**, Continental Army general who commanded troops in Boston and fought in Battle of Saratoga, Battle of White Plains, and Battle of Yorktown
- ★ **Joseph Palmer**, head of Watertown Committee of Correspondence, sent a message about the 1775 Lexington and Concord conflicts to Connecticut, New York, and major newspaper editors; his message explained that the American Revolution had begun
- ★ **Deborah Sampson**, fought in Continental Army disguised as a man during American Revolution, official Massachusetts state heroine
- ★ **Mercy Otis Warren**, attacked British policies in *Massachusetts Spy* articles

MICHIGAN

- ★ **Bridget Divers**, fought with husband, who suffered a leg wound, in First Michigan Cavalry; nursed wounded soldiers; once sneaked into enemy territory to rescue her captain's dead body, strapped the corpse to her horse, and rode 12 miles to find an embalmer and a coffin
- ★ **Sarah Emma Edmonds**, woman who cut off her hair and disguised herself as a man to fight with the Union army; received pension

- ★ **"Gentle Annie" Etheridge**, accompanied Second and Third Michigan Infantry units in the Civil War as a vivandiére (woman with camp and nurse duties who didn't disguise herself)
- ★ **Nancy Harkness Love**, created the Women's Auxiliary Ferrying Squadron (WAFS, later called Women's Air Force Service Pilots WASPS) to transport military supplies in World War II, founded Vassar College flight school
- ★ **Julia Wheelock**, "Michigan's Florence Nightingale" who nursed wounded Civil War troops, worked with Michigan Relief Association, raised money to support war effort; author

MINNESOTA

- ★ **The Andrews Sisters**, harmonious vocal trio that entertained U.S. troops and Americans during World War II; gave hope and encouragement to a war-torn nation
- ★ **Warren Earl Burger**, U.S. Supreme Court chief justice, presided over segregation cases
- ★ **William Orville Douglas**, U.S. Supreme Court justice (served longest term in history 1939-1975), author of 30 books on law and nature, fought for freedom of speech
- ★ **Lauris Norstad**, Supreme Allied Commander of NATO forces (1956-63)

MISSISSIPPI

- ★ **William Barksdale**, Confederate Brigadier General; when he died at the Battle of Gettysburg in 1863 his favorite hunting dog refused to leave his grave and also died
- ★ **Gen. John C. Pemberton**, led Confederate troops into Battle of Vicksburg (50,000 casualties) and surrendered to General Ulysses S. Grant on July 4, 1863
- ★ **Chief Pushmataha**, Choctaw chief who fought as a colonel in Battle of New Orleans; buried with full military honors in the Congressional Cemetery in Washington, D.C.
- ★ **John Anthony Quitman**, political leader, led volunteer troops in Mexican American War
- ★ **Gen. Eleazor W. Ripley**, War of 1812 hero, Congressional Medal of Honor recipient
- ★ **Sgt. Henry J. Tudury**, most decorated World War I soldier from Mississippi

MISSOURI

- ★ **Martha "Calamity Jane" Cannary Burke**, frontier scout for General George Custer in 1870, rural mail carrier, prospector, saved life of Captain Egan in Wyoming during Indian ambush, expert shooter and rider
- ★ **Gen. John "Black Jack" Pershing**, U.S. army general, commanded American Expeditionary Forces (AEF) in World War I, led campaign into Mexico to find revolutionary Pancho Villa, received Pulitzer Prize in history
- ★ **Wrinkles**, World War II canine messenger for Sgt. Archie Boyd, sniper from Grant City who fought in France

MONTANA

- ★ **Plenty Coups**, Crow Indian leader, U.S. Army scout, represented Native Americans at the Tomb of the Unknown Soldier dedication ceremony
- ★ **Michael Joseph Mansfield**, U.S. senator and representative, served longest term in history as Senate majority leader (1961-76), perhaps Montana's greatest politician
- ★ **Jeanette Rankin**, social reformer and women's suffragist, U.S. representative, first woman to ever hold a U.S. Congress seat

★ **Charles M. Russell**, Montana artist, created *Lewis and Clark Meeting Indians at Ross' Hole* painting, which hangs in the state capitol

NEBRASKA

★ **Gerald Ford**, 38th U.S. president, U.S Naval officer in World War II, U.S. representative
★ **Robert Kerrey**, earned Congressional Medal of Honor for Vietnam service, governor of Nebraska, U.S. senator
★ **John Lajba**, artist, created six bronze figures for World War II 50th anniversary memorial in Heartland of America Park

NEVADA

★ **Christopher "Kit" Carson**, frontiersman who guided John C. Frémont's expedition through Nevada, namesake of Carson City
★ **William Morris Stewart**, U.S. senator, wrote final version of the 15th Amendment

NEW HAMPSHIRE

★ **Josiah Barlett**, signed Declaration of Independence, physician, jurist, governor of New Hampshire
★ **Amos Barrett**, young minuteman who fought against British troops at the Battle of Concord
★ **Salmon Portland Chase**, U.S. Supreme Court chief justice, portrait on U.S. $10,000 bill, U.S. secretary of state, U.S. senator, governor of Ohio, U.S. secretary of the treasury, created basis for present national banking system
★ **Henry Dearborn**, Revolutionary War captain, U.S. secretary of war, major general in War of 1812
★ **Daniel Chester French**, sculpted Minute Man of Concord and Lincoln Memorial statue in Washington D.C.
★ **John Langdon**, Continental Congress and Constitutional Convention delegate, signed U.S. Constitution, governor of New Hampshire, U.S. senator, merchant
★ **Thaddeus S.C. Lowe**, inventor, scientist, led balloon force during Civil War
★ **John Sullivan**, Continental Congress delegate, led colonists in one of the first Revolutionary War attacks against the British, governor of New Hampshire, led state effort to ratify U.S. Constitution
★ **Meschech Weare**, first governor of New Hampshire during Revolutionary War, U.S. Supreme Court chief justice
★ **William Whipple**, Revolutionary War general, Continental Congress delegate, signed Declaration of Independence
★ **Christa McAuliffe**, was selected as the primary candidate for the NASA teacher in space project. She planned on teaching the first lessons taught from space. Moments after take-off, the space shuttle *Challenger* exploded killing everyone on board.

NEW JERSEY

★ **William Bainbridge**, commander of *USS Constitution* during War of 1812
★ **Elias Boudinot**, American Revolutionary patriot, president of Continental Congress
★ **David Brearly**, helped draft the U.S. Constitution

- ★ **Abraham Clark**, signed Declaration of Independence
- ★ **Stephen Crane**, international war journalist, novelist, authored *The Red Badge of Courage*
- ★ **James Lawrence**, naval captain, killed in battle, who said "Don't give up the ship" during the War of 1812
- ★ **Daniel Morgan**, U.S. congressman and Continental Army general who fought in Battle of Quebec, Siege of Boston, Battle of Saratoga, and Battle of Cowpens
- ★ **Thomas M. Peterson**, first African American to vote after 15th Amendment passage
- ★ **Gen. Norman Schwarzkopf Jr.**, led U.S. forces in Persian Gulf War

NEW MEXICO

- ★ **Manuel Chavez**, army scout and soldier, fought at Glorieta Pass
- ★ **Stephen Watts Kearny**, commander of the U.S. Army of the West during Mexican American War, led forces that occupied New Mexico and California

NEW YORK

- ★ **Mathew B. Brady**, photographer who documented the Civil War on film
- ★ **George Clinton**, soldier, governor of New York, U.S. vice president
- ★ **Lemuel Cook**, oldest surviving veteran of the Revolutionary War, aged 107 (as of 2003)
- ★ **James Forrestal**, secretary of U.S. Navy, first U.S. secretary of defense, helped build U.S. fleet into world's largest navy
- ★ **Horatio Gates**, English immigrant who became a major general in the Continental Army during Revolutionary War, retired in New York
- ★ **Rudy Giuliani**, beloved mayor of New York City, provided leadership in the midst of crisis following terrorist attacks on September 11, 2001
- ★ **John Jay**, first U.S. Supreme Court chief justice, helped negotiate Treaty of Paris to end American Revolution
- ★ **Gouverneur Morris**, U.S. senator, helped draft the U.S. Constitution
- ★ **Norman Rockwell**, classic American artist known for his *Saturday Evening Post* magazine covers, including the famous "Four Freedoms" painting
- ★ **Elihu Root**, U.S. secretary of war, U.S. secretary of state, U.S. senator, helped plan League of Nations' World Court, earned Nobel Peace Prize

NORTH CAROLINA

- ★ **Penelope Barker**, Edenton colonist who promoted the "tea party" protest of British tax
- ★ **William Hooper**, member of Continental Congress, signer of Declaration of Independence
- ★ **James Iredell**, encouraged North Carolina to ratify U.S. Constitution, original U.S. Supreme Court justice
- ★ **Dolley Payne Todd Madison**, one of the most important and influential women of her time, beloved First Lady of President James Madison; rescued a famous portrait of George Washington by cutting it from its frame when the British attacked Washington, D.C. by surprise; she saved her caged parrot too!

NORTH DAKOTA

- ★ **Robert Henry Bahmer**, head of National Archives and Records Administration who directed four presidential libraries
- ★ **Brynhild Haugland**, served as North Dakota legislator for 50 years
- ★ **Gen. Harold K. Johnson**, U.S. Army general, U.S. Army Chief of Staff, survived Bataan Death March during World War II
- ★ **Gen. David C. Jones**, U.S. Air Force general, chairman of Joint Chiefs of Staff, chief military advisor to the president, U.S. secretary of defense
- ★ **Admiral William Owens**, U.S. Navy officer, vice-chairman of Joint Chiefs of Staff

OHIO

- ★ **Johnny Clem**, nine-year-old Union army drummer from Newark who rallied troops
- ★ **John Glenn**, Marine colonel, U.S. senator, astronaut, oldest person to fly in space, first ` American to orbit the earth
- ★ **Maya Ting Lin**, designed Vietnam Veterans Memorial in Washington, D.C.

OKLAHOMA

- ★ **Angie Debo**, patriotic author of 13 state history books, known as "First Lady of Oklahoma History"
- ★ **William Murray**, governor of Oklahoma; helped improve unemployment during the Depression and donated part of his own salary to feed the hungry

OREGON

- ★ **Dr. John McLoughlin**, "Father of Oregon" who helped pioneers and missionaries settle in Oregon, founded Oregon City in 1842
- ★ **Richard Kelley Turner**, U.S. Navy admiral, planned and led American assaults in the Pacific during World War II

PENNSYLVANIA

- ★ **Gen. Alexander Haig Jr.**, U.S. Army four-star general, White House chief of staff, supreme commander of NATO forces in Europe, U.S. secretary of state
- ★ **Gen. Winfield S. Hancock**, Union general, played important role at Battle of Gettysburg
- ★ **Jonathan Harned**, officer in Pennsylvania militia during Revolutionary War
- ★ **Daniel Roberdeau**, brigadier general in Pennsylvania militia in Revolutionary War, began duty on July 4, 1776

RHODE ISLAND

- ★ **George M. Cohan**, Providence native who wrote patriotic songs including, "Over There," "Yankee Doodle," and "You're a Grand Old Flag"
- ★ **Gen. Nathanael Greene**, Continental general in American Revolution, led 1,000 troops from Rhode Island to Boston to join Continental Army
- ★ **Esek Hopkins**, commander-in-chief of Continental Navy
- ★ **Stephen Hopkins**, governor of Rhode Island colony in mid 1700s, member of Continental Congress, signer of Declaration of Independence

- ★ **Julia Ward Howe**, poet, wrote "Battle Hymn of the Republic" text, founded New England Woman Suffrage Association, *Woman's Journal* editor
- ★ **Matthew Calbraith Perry**, naval officer, fought in War of 1812 and Mexican American War in 1847, opened diplomatic and trade relations with Japan in 1853
- ★ **Oliver Hazard Perry**, commanded fleet of ships in War of 1812, won Battle of Lake Erie
- ★ **Gilbert Stuart**, portrait artist who painted first five U.S. presidents
- ★ **Abraham Whipple**, commanded two ships in American Revolution, which launched the U.S. Navy

SOUTH CAROLINA

- ★ **Pierce Butler**, Irish immigrant, signed U.S. Constitution, American Revolution patriot leader, first U.S. senator from South Carolina
- ★ **Elijah Clarke**, brigadier general, served with Andrew Pickens and Thomas Sumter, American Revolution patriot militia
- ★ **Christopher "Flame of Liberty" Gadsden**, Revolutionary War patriot
- ★ **Gen. Wade Hampton**, noted Confederate general, U.S. senator, late 1800s governor of South Carolina
- ★ **Thomas Heyward**, signer of the Declaration of Independence, Continental Congress member
- ★ **Henry Laurens**, member and president of the Continental Congress, negotiated the peace treaty that ended the Revolution
- ★ **Francis "Swamp Fox" Marion**, used guerrilla tactics successfully against British forces during the American Revolution
- ★ **Arthur Middleton**, Continental Congress member, signed Declaration of Independence, designed South Carolina state seal
- ★ **Robert Mills**, influential architect in early U.S. history, designed National Treasury, Washington Monument, U.S. post office, U.S. patent office
- ★ **Rebecca Brewton Motte**, American Revolution patriot, negotiated British surrender at "Fort Motte"
- ★ **William Moultrie**, major general in Continental Army, successfully defended Charleston against British attack, governor of South Carolina
- ★ **Andrew Pickens**, Revolutionary War commander, decisive leader in Battle of Cowpens
- ★ **Charles Pinckney**, Continental Congress member, helped draft and form U.S. Constitution, three-time governor of South Carolina
- ★ **Thomas "The Gamecock" Sumter**, used guerrilla tactics successfully against British forces during American Revolution, U.S. senator
- ★ **James "Strom" Thurmond**, longest-serving U.S. senator in history, governor of South Carolina, presidential candidate, died at age 100
- ★ **William Barret Travis**, lieutenant colonel in U.S. Army (cavalry), died defending Alamo

SOUTH DAKOTA

- ★ **Gutzon Borglum**, sculpted bust of Abraham Lincoln in U.S. Capitol rotunda and carved presidents on Mount Rushmore
- ★ **Gen. George Armstrong Custer**, died in Battle of Little Big Horn

- ★ **Joseph J. Foss**, World War II aviator, awarded the Congressional Medal of Honor and Distinguished Flying Cross

TENNESSEE

- ★ **Hattie Caraway**, first woman elected to U.S. Senate, to head a Senate committee, and to preside over a U.S. Senate session
- ★ **Samuel Powhatan Carter**, only American to serve as a U.S. Navy admiral and U.S. Army general
- ★ **John Sevier**, first governor of Tennessee (served for six terms), U.S. congressman, patriot militia member

TEXAS

- ★ **Stephen F. Austin**, "Father of Texas" and influential politician
- ★ **David Crockett**, frontiersman, politician, military scout; led group of volunteers in the Texas Revolution and was killed in 1836 defending the Alamo
- ★ **Sarah Dodson**, created a lone star flag for her husband's militia company
- ★ **Clara Driscoll**, member of the Daughters of the Revolution, helped save the Alamo from destruction and promoted its preservation
- ★ **Sam Houston**, first president of the Republic of Texas, U.S. senator, Texas army major general (captured Santa Anna), governor of Texas and Tennessee; Nashville attorney general
- ★ **Mirabeau B. Lamar**, "Father of Education," president of Republic of Texas
- ★ **Audie Murphy**, most decorated American soldier of World War II; wounded three times, earned 33 awards and medals, including the Medal of Honor, before the age of 21
- ★ **Admiral Chester W. Nimitz**, commander-in-chief of Pacific Fleet during World II, class of aircraft carriers was named for him

UTAH

- ★ **Benjamin O. Davis Sr.**, first African American general in U.S. history, served at Fort Duchesne after Spanish-American War
- ★ **George H. Dern**, governor of Utah, U.S. secretary of war
- ★ **Edwin Jacob Garn**, naval pilot, mayor of Salt Lake City, U.S. senator, flew aboard *Discovery* space shuttle in 1985

VERMONT

- ★ **Ira Allen**, wrote preamble to the constitution of the independent state of Vermont, brother of Ethan Allen, founded the University of Vermont, served in the state legislature
- ★ **Warren Austin**, U.S. senator, headed first U.S. delegation to United Nations
- ★ **Thomas Chittenden**, helped write Vermont's constitution, first state governor of Vermont
- ★ **George Dewey**, U.S. naval officer who served under Admiral Farragut in Civil War, commanded Asian squadron during Spanish-American War
- ★ **Lemuel Haynes**, fought with Minutemen in 1775, fought with Ethan Allen at Fort Ticonderoga battle
- ★ **Samuel Herrick**, Revolutionary War officer who fought at Battle of Bennington, gained control of Lake George, forced the British to evacuate Fort Ticonderoga, and captured Skeenesborough, New York

- ★ **Matthew Lyon**, Green Mountain Boys officer, U.S. representative
- ★ **Justin Smith Morrill**, U.S. representative (served 44 consecutive years), sponsored Land Grant Colleges Act of 1862, and helped create Library of Congress and Washington Monument
- ★ **Hiram Powers**, sculpted Benjamin Franklin and Thomas Jefferson statues for U.S. Capitol
- ★ **Ann Story**, "Mother of the Green Mountain Boys," her home was used as a message drop and shelter for patriots during the American Revolution
- ★ **J.E.B. Stuart**, Confederate Army general, fought in U.S. cavalry, fought in First Battle of Manassas (Bull Run) and Battle of Gettysburg, died in battle
- ★ **Sally Louisa Tompkins**, nursed hundreds of wounded Confederate soldiers after First Battle of Manassas (Bull Run); her sanitary methods resulted in a higher rate of patient success and honor from Confederate President Jefferson Davis
- ★ **Seth Warner**, helped found Green Mountain Boys and led them after the British captured Ethan Allen; led forces that captured Crown Point in 1775 and helped Gen. John Stark plan the Battle of Bennington, captured ships

VIRGINIA

- ★ **Carter Braxton**, Revolutionary War patriot
- ★ **Moses Jacob Ezekiel**, sculpted monument to Confederate dead in Arlington National Cemetery
- ★ **Maggie Higgins**, first woman to win Pulitzer Prize for international reporting; covered Allied liberation of Dachau during World War II, Nuremberg Trials, Vietnam War, Korean War; wife and daughter of soldiers; buried in Arlington Cemetery
- ★ **Francis Lightfoot Lee**, signed Declaration of Independence, Virginia House of Burgesses member
- ★ **John Marshall**, U.S. Supreme Court chief justice, fought in Continental Army in Revolutionary War; lieutenant of Culpeper Minute Men, organized in 1775
- ★ **Lewis F. Powell Jr.**, U.S. Supreme Court justice, colonel
- ★ **Edmund Jennings Randolph**, first U.S. attorney general, General Washington's aide-de-camp, Continental Congress delegate, Constitutional Convention member, governor of Virginia, U.S. secretary of state
- ★ **Mary Martha Reid**, nurse who cared for Civil War soldiers, first chapter of the U.S. Daughters of the Confederacy was named after her
- ★ **Winfield Scott**, War of 1812 hero
- ★ **Mollie Tynes**, young Confederate who rode all night to alert mountain families of an impending Yankee attack on the salt mines of Wytheville; her brave ride resulted in local defense effort which saved town and mines
- ★ **William Washington**, Continental Army brigadier general who fought in Battles of Trenton, Monck's Corner, Cowpens, and Guilford Courthouse

WASHINGTON

- ★ **George Bush**, fought with Andrew Jackson at the Battle of New Orleans
- ★ **Sam Hill**, lawyer, businessman, diplomat; designed and built Peace Arch, a memorial to honor World War I soldiers
- ★ **Gen. Jonathan Mahew Wainwright**, U.S. Army general in World War II

WEST VIRGINIA

- ★ **Ann Bailey**, scout and sharpshooter nicknamed "Mad Ann" Bailey after riding 100 miles through dense underbrush to deliver gunpowder to a fort during an Indian siege
- ★ **John William Davis**, lawyer and U.S. representative from Clarksburg; argued more cases before the U.S. Supreme Court than any other attorney
- ★ **Francis H. Pierpont**, governor of the Restored Government of Virginia in 1861, helped form the independent state of West Virginia, "Father of West Virginia"
- ★ **Daddy Smith**, slave who singlehandedly defended a key wall at Fort Henry in a major 1777 battle
- ★ **Chuck Yeager**, shot down 13 enemy aircraft during his military career in World War II; first person to travel faster than the speed of sound (via aircraft)

WISCONSIN

- ★ **Dr. William Beaumont**, U.S. Army surgeon
- ★ **Richard Ira Bong**, World War II pilot, awarded the Medal of Honor
- ★ **Mildred Harnach**, organized resistance groups and sent intelligence information to Allies during World War II; executed by Nazis
- ★ **Cordelia Harvey**, humanitarian, founded military hospitals in Civil War, governor's wife
- ★ **Robert M. La Follette Sr.**, founder of Progressive Movement, U.S. representative and senator, lawyer, governor of Wisconsin
- ★ **Michael Red Cloud Jr.**, soldier awarded Medal of Honor posthumously for bravery in Korean War
- ★ **William H. Rehnquist**, U.S. Supreme Court justice, chief justice; served in U.S. Air Force

WYOMING

- ★ **Willis Van Devanter**, lawyer, chief justice of Wyoming Territory, U.S. circuit judge, U.S. Supreme Court justice
- ★ **"Grandma" Eliza Swain**, first woman in U.S. history to vote in a general election
- ★ **Francis Emroy Warren**, Civil War veteran, governor of Wyoming, U.S. senator for 37 years

Presidents of the...

GEORGE WASHINGTON
(b. 1732, d. 1799)
No party affiliation
Term: 1789-1797

JOHN ADAMS
(b. 1735, d. 1826)
No party affiliation
Term: 1797-1801

THOMAS JEFFERSON
(b. 1743, d. 1826)
Democratic-Republican
Term: 1801-1809

JAMES MADISON
(b. 1751, d. 1836)
Democratic-Republican
Term: 1809-1817

JAMES MONROE
(b. 1758, d. 1831)
Democratic-Republican
Term: 1817-1825

JOHN QUINCY ADAMS
(b. 1767, d. 1848)
Democratic-Republican
Term: 1825-1829

ANDREW JACKSON
(b. 1767, d. 1845)
Democratic
Term: 1829-1837

MARTIN VAN BUREN
(b. 1782, d. 1862)
Democratic
Term: 1837-1841

WILLIAM HENRY HARRISON
(b. 1773, d. 1841)
Whig
Term: 1841-1841

JOHN TYLER
(b. 1790, d. 1862)
Whig
Term: 1841-1845

JAMES KNOX POLK
(b. 1795, d. 1849)
Democratic
Term: 1845-1849

ZACHARY TAYLOR
(b. 1784, d. 1850)
Whig
Term: 1849-1850

MILLARD FILLMORE
(b. 1800, d. 1874)
Whig
Term: 1850-1853

FRANKLIN PIERCE
(b. 1804, d. 1869)
Democratic
Term: 1853-1857

JAMES BUCHANAN
(b. 1791, d. 1868)
Democratic
Term: 1857-1861

ABRAHAM LINCOLN
(b. 1809, d. 1865)
Republican
Term: 1861-1865

ANDREW JOHNSON
(b. 1808, d. 1875)
National Union
Term: 1865-1869

ULYSSES S. GRANT
(b. 1822, d. 1885)
Republican
Term: 1869-1877

RUTHERFORD B. HAYES
(b. 1822, d. 1893)
Republican
Term: 1877-1881

JAMES A. GARFIELD
(b. 1831, d. 1881)
Republican
Term: 1881-1881

CHESTER A. ARTHUR
(b. 1830, d. 1886)
Republican
Term: 1881-1885

GROVER CLEVELAND
(b. 1837, d. 1908)
Democratic
Term: 1885-1889

BENJAMIN HARRISON
(b. 1833, d. 1901)
Republican
Term: 1889-1893

GROVER CLEVELAND
(b. 1837, d. 1908)
Democratic
Term: 1893-1897

United States of America

WILLIAM MCKINLEY
(b. 1843, d. 1901)
Republican
Term: 1897-1901

THEODORE ROOSEVELT
(b. 1858, d. 1919)
Republican
Term: 1901-1909

WILLIAM H. TAFT
(b. 1857, d. 1930)
Republican
Term: 1909-1913

WOODROW WILSON
(b. 1856, d. 1924)
Democratic
Term: 1913-1921

WARREN G. HARDING
(b. 1865, d. 1923)
Republican
Term: 1921-1923

CALVIN COOLIDGE
(b. 1872, d. 1933)
Republican
Term: 1923-1929

HERBERT C. HOOVER
(b. 1874, d. 1964)
Republican
Term: 1929-1933

FRANKLIN D. ROOSEVELT
(b. 1882, d. 1945)
Democratic
Term: 1933-1945

HARRY S. TRUMAN
(b. 1884, d. 1972)
Democratic
Term: 1945-1953

DWIGHT D. EISENHOWER
(b. 1890, d. 1969)
Republican
Term: 1953-1961

JOHN F. KENNEDY
(b. 1917, d. 1963)
Democratic
Term: 1961-1963

LYNDON B. JOHNSON
(b. 1908, d. 1973)
Democratic
Term: 1963-1969

RICHARD M. NIXON
(b. 1913, d. 1994)
Republican
Term: 1969-1974

GERALD R. FORD
(b. 1913-)
Republican
Term: 1974-1977

JAMES E. CARTER
(b. 1924-)
Democratic
Term: 1977-1981

RONALD W. REAGAN
(b. 1911-2004)
Republican
Term: 1981-1989

GEORGE H.W. BUSH
(b. 1924-) Republican
Term: 1989-1993

WILLIAM J. CLINTON
(b. 1946-) Democratic
Term: 1993-2001

GEORGE W. BUSH
(b. 1946-) Republican
Term: January 20, 2001 –

Signers of the Declaration of Independence

Connecticut:	Roger Sherman, Samuel Huntington, William Williams, Oliver Wolcott
Delaware:	Caesar Rodney, George Read, Thomas McKean
Georgia:	Button Gwinnett, Lyman Hall, George Walton
Maryland:	Samuel Chase, William Paca, Thomas Stone, Charles Carrol
Massachusetts:	John Hancock, Samuel Adams, John Adams, Robert Treat Paine, Elbridge Gerry
New Hampshire:	Josiah Bartlett, William Whipple, Matthew Thornton
New Jersey:	Richard Stockton, John Witherspoon, Francis Hopkinson, John Hart, Abraham Clark
New York:	William Floyd, Philip Livingston, Francis Lewis, Lewis Morris
North Carolina:	William Hooper, Joseph Hewes, John Penn
South Carolina:	Edward Rutledge, Thomas Heyward, Thomas Lynch, Arthur Middleton
Pennsylvania:	Robert Morris, Benjamin Rush, Benjamin Franklin, John Morton, George Clymer, James Smith, George Taylor, James Wilson, George Ross
Rhode Island:	Stephen Hopkins, William Ellery
Virginia:	George Wythe, Richard Henry Lee, Thomas Jefferson, Benjamin Harrison, Thomas Nelson Jr., Francis Lightfoot Lee, Carter Braxton

Signers of the U.S. Constitution

Connecticut:	Roger Sherman, William Samuel Johnson
Delaware:	George Read, Gunning Bedford Jr., John Dickinson, Richard Bassett, Jacob Broom
Georgia:	William Few, Abraham Baldwin
Maryland:	James McHenry, Daniel Carroll, Dan of St. Thomas Jenifer
Massachusetts:	Rufus King, Nathaniel Gorham
New Hampshire:	John Langdon, Nicholas Gilman
New Jersey:	William Livingston, David Brearley, William Paterson, Jonathan Dayton
New York:	Alexander Hamilton
North Carolina:	William Blount, Richard Dobbs Spaight, Hugh Williamson
Pennsylvania:	Benjamin Franklin, Thomas Mifflin, Robert Morris, George Clymer, Thomas FitzSimons, Jared Ingersoll, Gouverneur Morris, James Wilson
South Carolina:	John Rutledge, Charles Cotesworth Pinckney, Charles Pinckney, Pierce Butler
Virginia:	John Blair, James Madison Jr.